Because I Love You!

Too often, we leave the vital things unsaid, so I wanted you to know:

I love you, and I have felt loved by you. Every memory I have of you is, and always will be, cherished.

I have been blessed to have you in my life. The memories I have of you and the lessons I have learned from you, the times we have laughed to-gether and we have cried together, the good times and the struggles: They are part of my life and who I am, and I would not trade them for anything.

Thank you for being you and for not just being part of my life, but for being part of who I am.

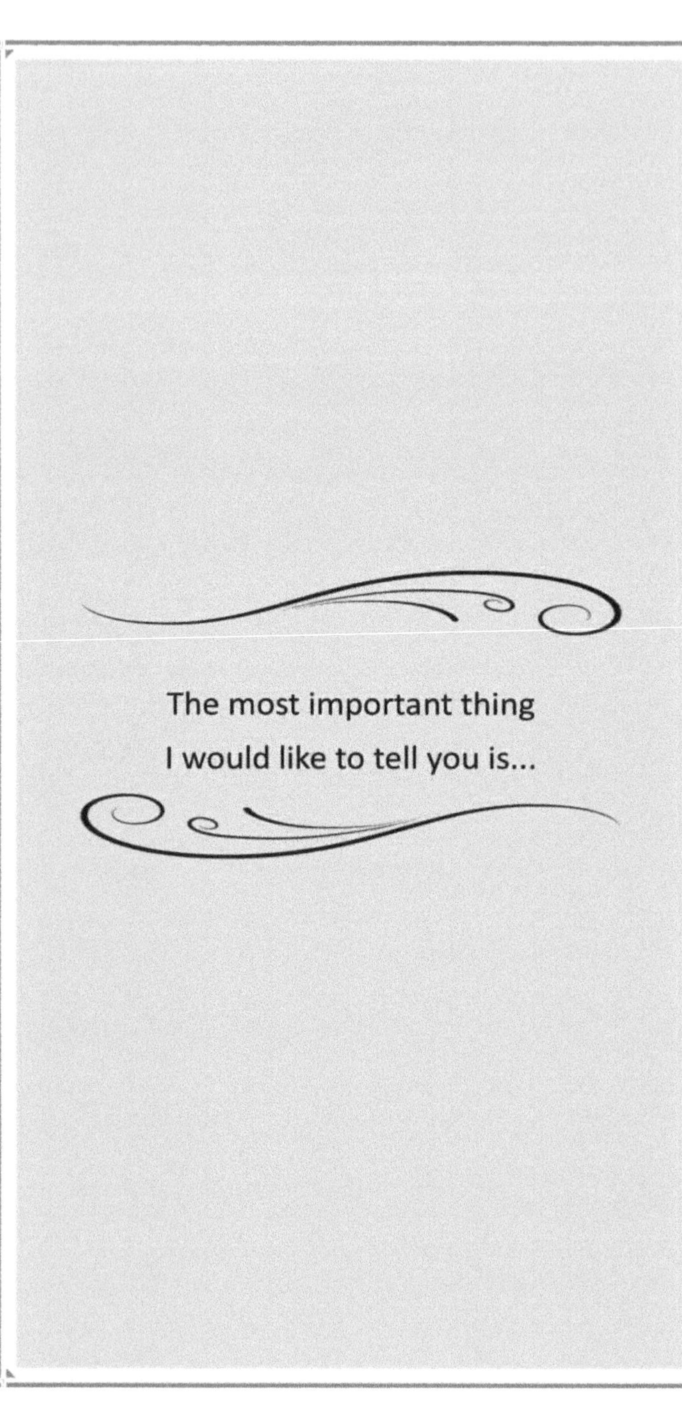

The most important thing
I would like to tell you is...

I will always admire you because...

We have shared laughter and love in good
times and bad. There are so many
things that make me think of you
and our times together.

These are the heartfelt times I

hold on to...

When I think of you, so many
things make me smile.

The ones that make me smile no matter
what I am going through are...

____

____

____

____

____

____

____

____

____

____

____

I would not be
the person I
am today
without you.

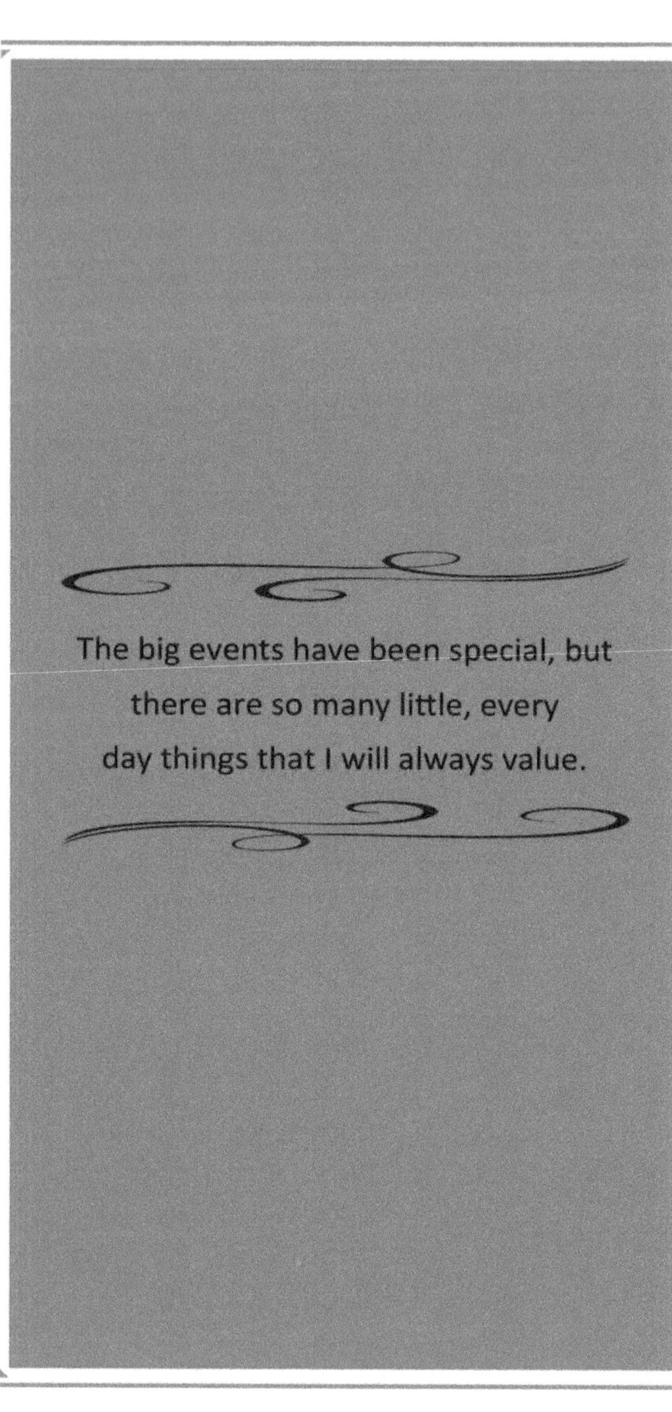

The big events have been special, but
there are so many little, every
day things that I will always value.

My favorites of these are...

Places remind me of my happiest
memories. The places that make
me think of you include...

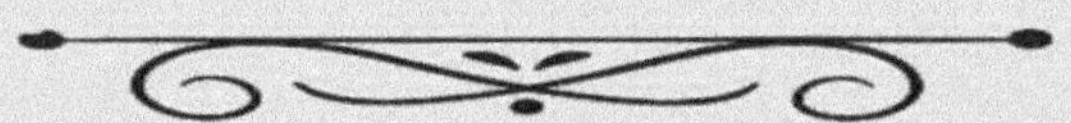

How you have lived has had even more
impact on my life than your words have.

These are the things about how you have
lived your life that have changed mine...

It might surprise you that one of
my favorite memories of you is...

You are a gift,

greater than a

new day.

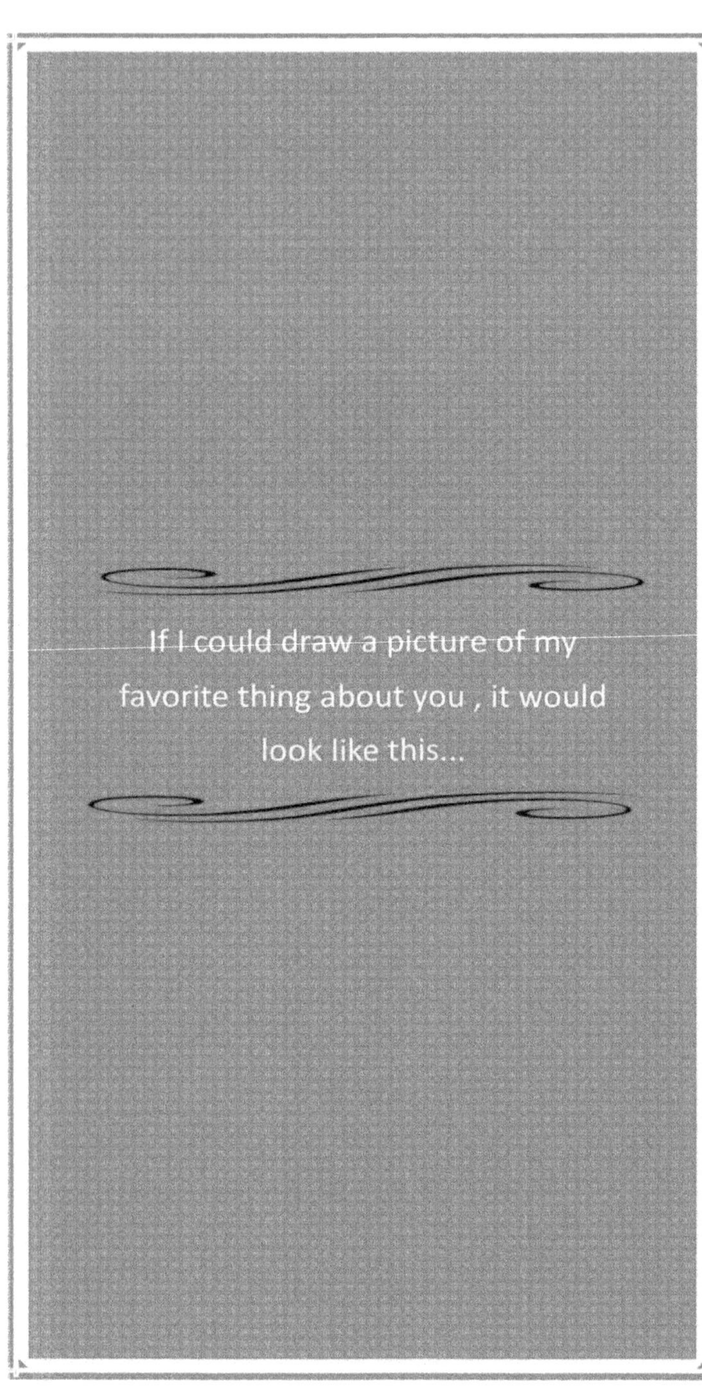
If I could draw a picture of my
favorite thing about you , it would
look like this...

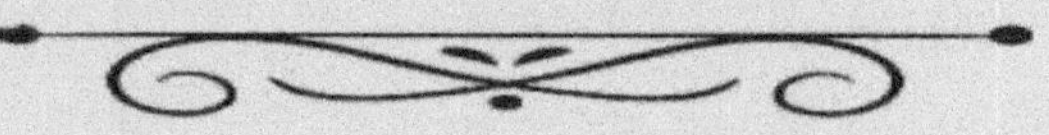

We haven't always agreed….

and that's okay.

These are some times I wish I
had listened sooner...

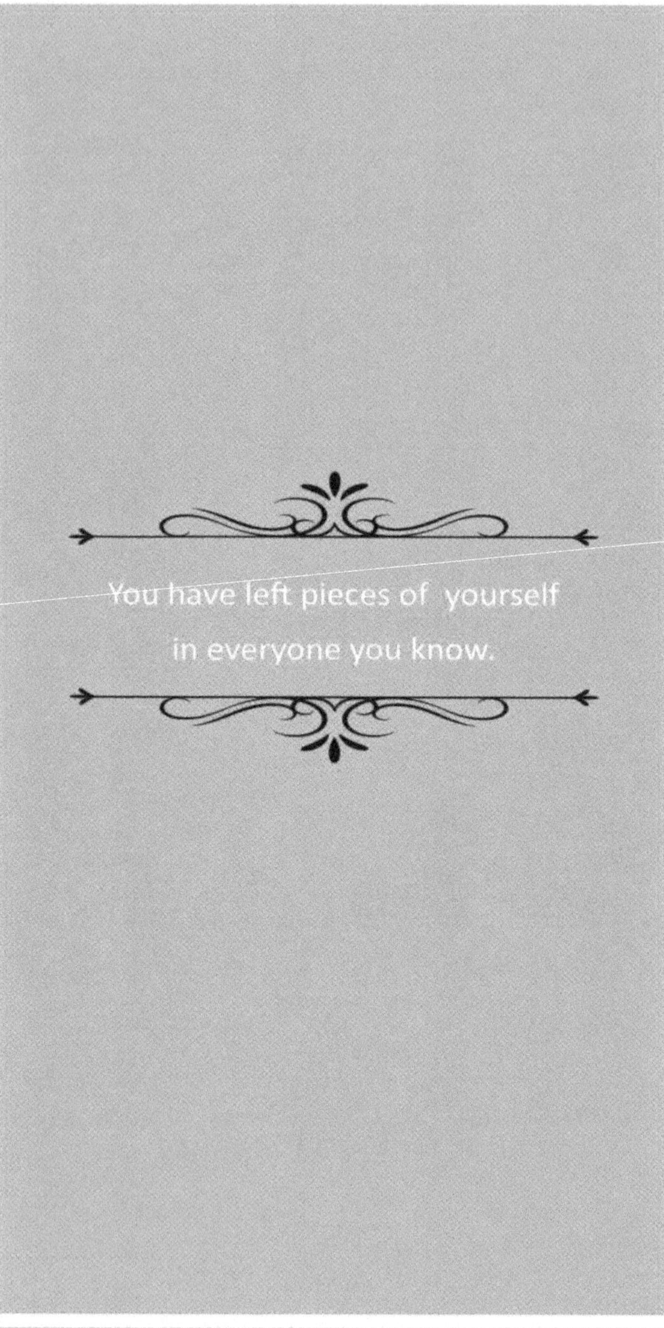

You have left pieces of yourself
in everyone you know.

This is what you have left in me...

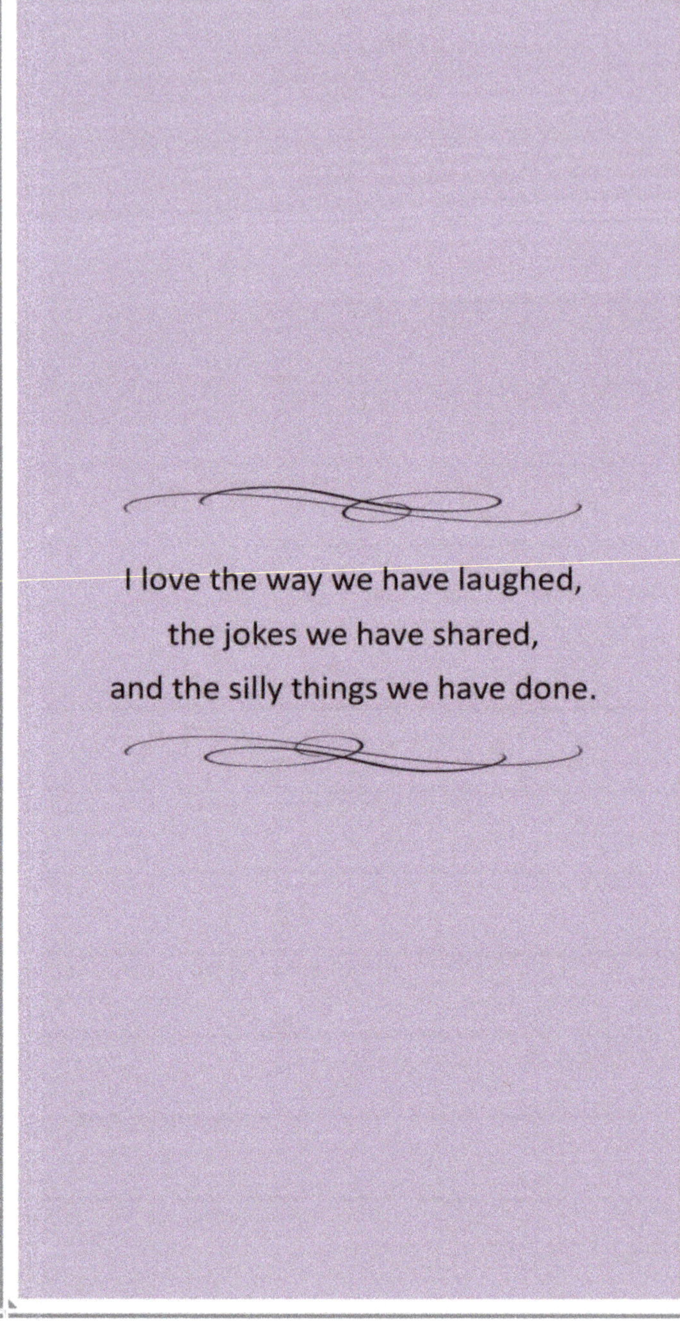

I love the way we have laughed,
the jokes we have shared,
and the silly things we have done.

These are some of my favorites...

Some people

make life better

for the people

around them.

Thank you for being one of them.

The greatest gift you have
given me is...

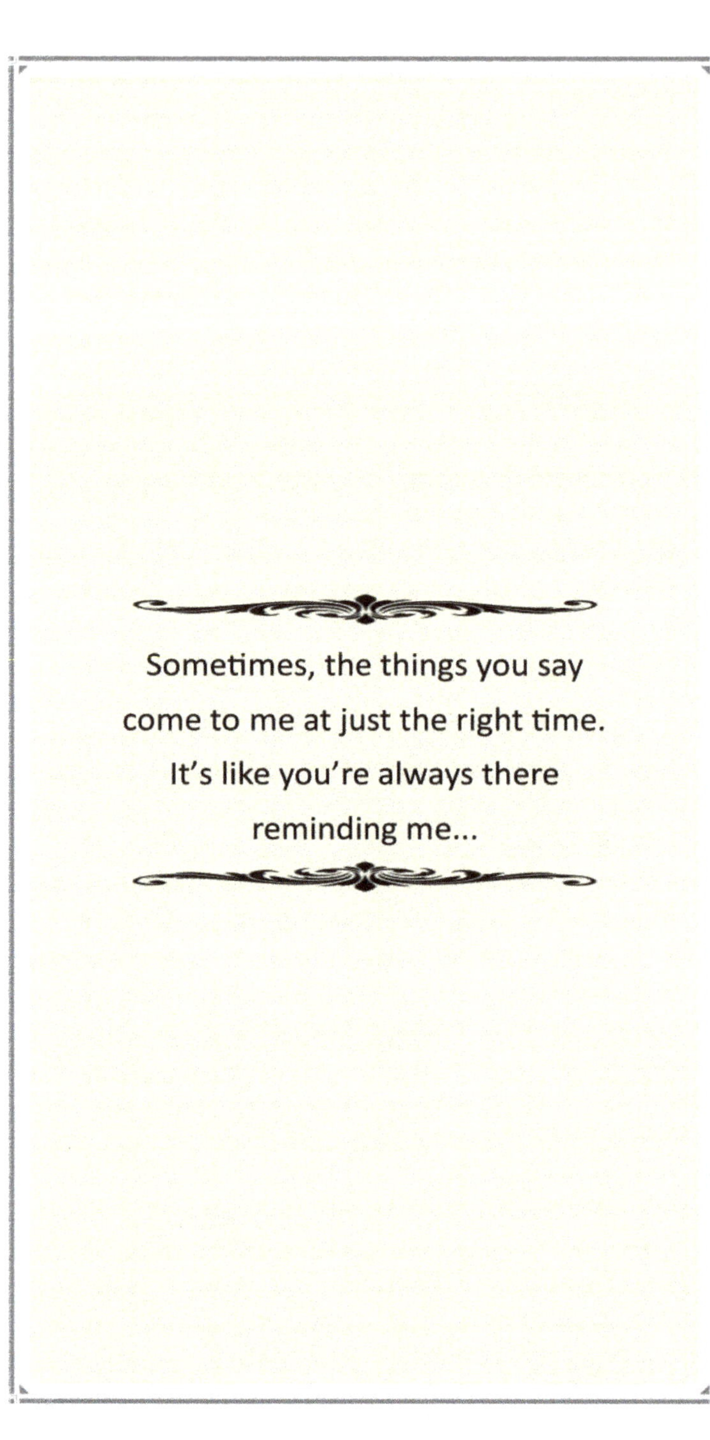

Sometimes, the things you say
come to me at just the right time.
It's like you're always there
reminding me...

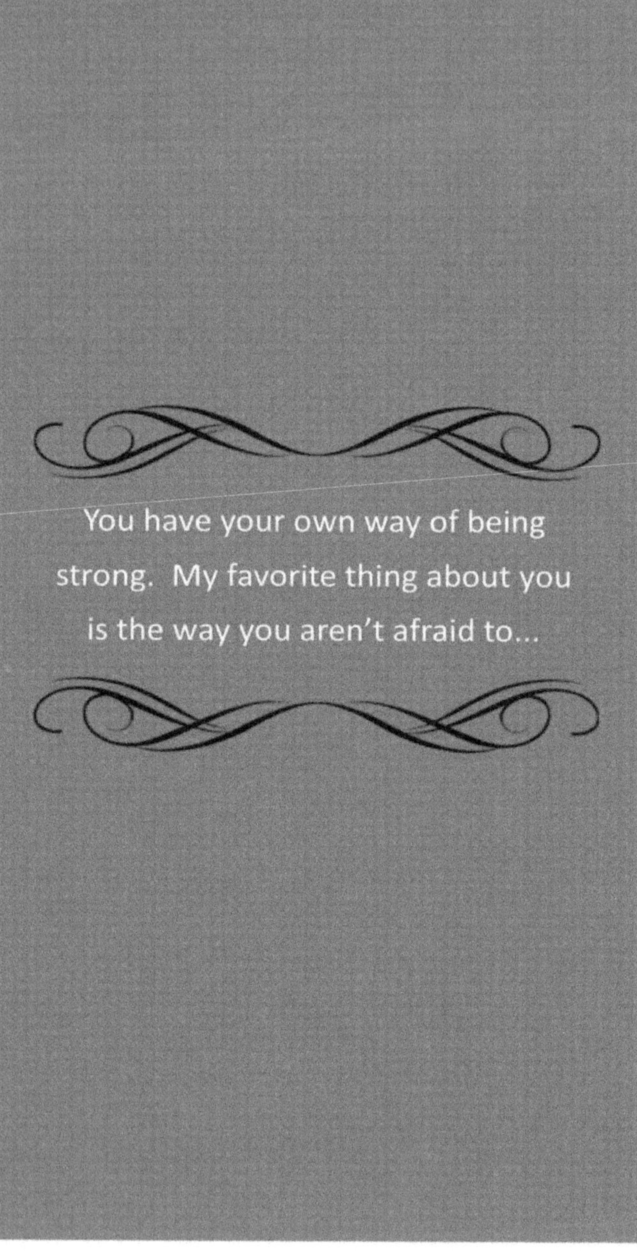
You have your own way of being
strong. My favorite thing about you
is the way you aren't afraid to...

I don't know how
you do it, but you always
manage to...

My Love Letter to You

Picture Pages

Shared History

A Few of Our Great Firsts

Obstacles We've Overcome

Opportunities I missed to
Thank You

The "I'm Glad We Did That" List

"Best of" Certificates

Certificate of Appreciation

This certifies that ________________________________

is the best ______________________________ by

virtue of ____

____.

Officially endorsed by.

____

This ________of ____________________20______

Certificate of Appreciation

This certifies that ________________________________

is the most likely to ______________________________

by virtue of ______________________________________

____.

Officially endorsed by.

____

This ________of ____________________20______

"Best of" Certificates

Certificate of Appreciation

This certifies that ________________________________

has the best taste in ________________________________

by virtue of ________________________________

________________________________.

Officially endorsed by.

____

This ________of ________________20____

Certificate of Appreciation

This certifies that ________________________________

is the chief executive of ________________________________

by virtue of ________________________________

________________________________.

Officially endorsed by.

____

This ________of ________________20____

"Best of" Certificates

Certificate of Appreciation

This certifies that ________________________________

is the undisputed champion of ___________

________________________________ by virtue of

________________________________.

Officially endorsed by.

____

This ________of ________________20_____

Certificate of Appreciation

This certifies that ________________________________

has blessed the life of ________________________________

through faithfulness, friendship, and truth
spoken with love, and will forever be held in
my heart and memories fondly.

Officially endorsed by.

____

This ________of ________________20_____

www.ingramcontent.com/pod-product-compliance
Lightning Source LLC
Chambersburg PA
CBHW050019040726
47599CB00014B/1453